CHILI PEPPER FINDS A HOME

CHILI PEPPER FINDS A HOME

BY

LOIS CHIPMAN-SULLIVAN

www.bookstandpublishing.com

Published by
Bookstand Publishing
Morgan Hill, CA 95037
3221_1

Copyright © 2010 by Lois Chipman-Sullivan
All rights reserved. No part of this publication may be reproduced or transmitted in any form or by any means, electronic or mechanical, including photocopy, recording, or any information storage and retrieval system, without permission in writing from the copyright owner.

ISBN 978-1-58909-806-0

Printed in the United States of America

My story is dedicated to all of my pet friends who have made me and my family so happy.

So, here is to Krystal, Timber, Soapy, Patches, Comet, Rusty, Ruby, Ike, Leo, Bailey, Boo, Bonzo, Josephine, Napoleon, Scooter, Brinney, Dutchey, Cesar, Shampoo, Snowball, Barney, Missy, Bandit, Princess, Chester, Blackie, Betsy, Biff, Bing, Trisha, Ajax, Christmas, Bullet, Pepper, Sandy, Petite, PJ, Stormy, Miss Kitty, Duchess, Brandy, Major, Moses, Corky and all the people who have loved them so much~

Your friend,

Chili Pepper Sullivan

A Puppy's Life

Page 1:

Hi, my name is Chili Pepper. This is my first day in my new home and I am just a little puppy who is kind of scared ~ what will it be like?

Page 2:

Will I be able to make friends?

Page 3:

I just came to my new home and I want to show you how much fun it is to live with friends. Comet and Patches were waiting for me!

Page 4:

Wow, look at the food here. I bet that I will have lots of good puppy dinners. My tummy feels good already!

Page 5:

Maybe I can find something I like all by myself.

Page 6:

I think this is how I get outside ~ I have my own little door that is special for me!

Page 7:

What do I see over there?

Page 8:

Do you think that other dog will play with me?

Page 9:

Oh, her name is Josephine! I think she likes me, we can play together!

Page 10:

Playing outside was really great fun. I think this is how I get back in the house. Do you think this is the way?

Page 11:

Sometimes I get really tired after I play outside and just need to take a little nap on my favorite rug that is just my size.

Page 12:

Oh boy, my new friend, Josephine and I like to take naps together sometimes. We have lots of fun together. She is like a Mom to me. What a great home this is!

Growing Up With My Friends!

Page 13:

Now that I have grown bigger, I can play a lot with my brother, Comet. He teaches me how to look for squirrels!

Page 14:

We play together and then have to take a nap. He is my Buddy!

Page 15:

I think I better go and check out what is happening outside ~ maybe there are some friends out there, too~

Page 16:

Sometimes the whole neighborhood wants me to come out and play!

Page 17:

Even Lily, she is a special friend who lives next door and lets me chase her all around the house when she comes to visit!

Page 18:

Ike and Leo, our kitten cousins, just like to stay home together most of the time but we always remember them, too!

I like it when my neighbor friends come over to play, too. This is Ruby and she like to dress up like a ballerina. She loves Halloween!

Page 20:

Barney and Missy always come over to watch and laugh!

Page 21:

While we are playing in the house, Ruby's big brother, Rusty, likes to cool off in the water. He likes to run around outside a lot!

Page 22:

Bailey lives in Pennsylvania so we just send pictures to each other. I know he likes to make friends with chickens!

Page 23:

Sometimes I like to play by myself. I like to play dress-up and see if my new friends can tell me who I am!

Page 24:

Sometimes, after we play, Josephine gets all tired out!

Page 25:

Sometimes, after we play, Comet gets me all tired out!

Page 26:

Sometimes, after we play, I just get tired all by myself!

Page 27:

When we are all asleep, our Gramma, Soapy, watches over us so we are safe.

Page 28:

My big sister, Patches, can sleep just about any place ~ and she snores, too!

Summertime in Maine ~ with More Friends!

Page 29:

When it is summertime, we go camping in Maine with our friends Boo and Bonzo. They are waiting for us today!

Page 30:

Maybe they think we are at this door ~ their Grandma, Old Dog Brinney, is watching too!

Page 31:

When we are in Maine, we go out in the woods to look for birds and squirrels. I have to wear my vest so I don't get lost.

Page 32:

What do you think? Does it look good? I like it!

I have to be careful when I am in the woods and always stay close to my friends.

Page 34:

Boo and I like to go down to the water and see what we can see. We wear sweaters when it gets cold!

Page 35:

After a long day of being outside, Boo and I like to lie in the sun and warm up.

Page 36:

After a day in the woods, Bonzo and Boo are still ready to run and play~

Page 37:

Now Boo is ready to take a nap with me.

Page 38:

Josephine waits in the house for us because she gets too tired sometimes and doesn't like to get her paws and nose dirty!

At night, in the woods, it can get cold and I need to snuggle.

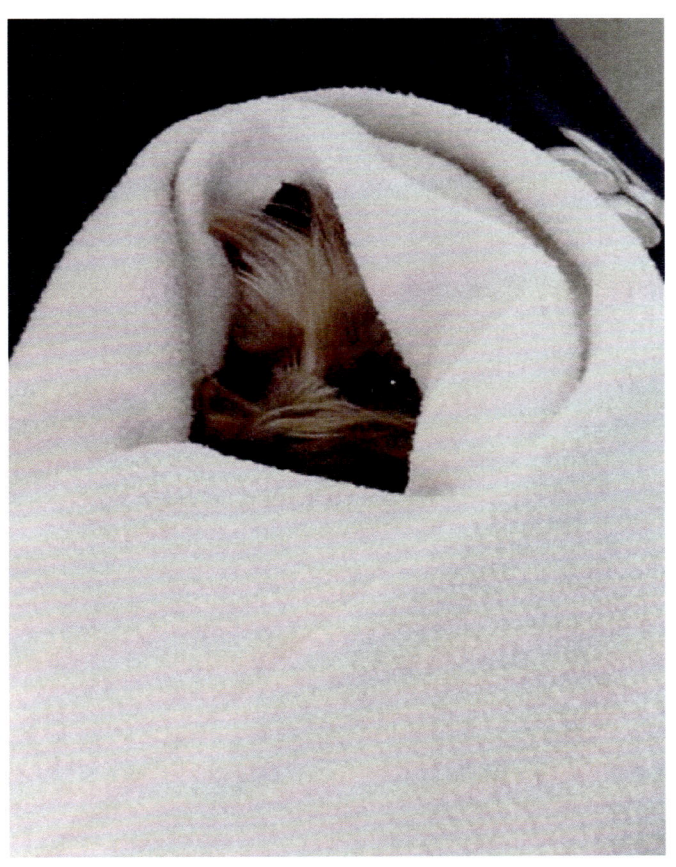

Page 40:

And Boo is tired, too~

Page 41:

An Old Dog Brinney is the most tired of all!

Page 42:

In the summertime there are extra special days to have fun. We like the 4th of July, too. We can get dressed up to have a party!

Winter Fun

Page 43:

In the winter time, we like to wait all together when it's time to go visiting especially when it's holiday time!

Page 44:

Here is my whole family ~ me, Josephine, Comet and Patches. We have fun all together as a happy family. We share our Christmas treats. How much fun it is when we are all together. We really like each other a lot!

When I go to my friend's house for Christmas, we get dressed up. Hey! It's a Party, Let's Wear Hats!

Page 46:

This is my cousin, Scooter, and he likes to bark a lot! We visit him at Christmas time, too!

Page 47:

Here is Scooter's Dad, Napoleon. Doesn't he look great! He's a really good Dad!

Page 48:

After a Holiday Party, we all need to take a nap together!

See how much fun it is to have family and friends and to share together. Come and visit me someday and I will share my fun with you, too!

Page 50:

It makes me happy to think you are my friend too. It's time to say good night. Your friend, Chili Pepper~